HEALING

YOUR

BROKEN HEART

21 Proven Steps To Cope With Heartbreak In Relationship, Recover From Its Pain And Happily Move On With Your Life

OGHOVEMU DANIEL OKPU

HEALING YOUR BROKEN HEART

21 Proven Steps To Cope With Heartbreak In Relationship, Recover From Its Pain And Happily Move On With Your Life

Copyright © 2019 by:
Oghovemu Daniel Okpu

Cover Design by: Josiah Apoi (+2349036375170)

WHAT PEOPLE ARE SAYING ABOUT THIS BOOK

I'm done reading this book and I can say it's indeed a heartbreak healing balm. The strategies shared in it are really helpful and they can work for all forms of heartbreak aside that of romatic relationship.

Ogheneochukome Judith Eghaghara

This book, "Healing Your Broken Heart" by Oghovemu Daniel Okpu is worth buying and reading. The book is very interesting and inspiring. The great words in it will grip and keep you turning the pages. It can inspire anyone no matter who you're.

Having read this book and found it a rich source of information that will not only help one recover from heartbreak, but also inspire anyone to aim higher, I therefore recommend it for everyone who desires to happily move on to achieve great things and live his/her best life.

Myra O. Oba

DEDICATION

This book, "HEALING YOUR BROKEN HEART" is dedicated to all those who are going through heartbreak, especially in relationship, and would have their broken hearts healed after reading it.

CONTENTS

INTRODUCTION

One of the things that people fear in relationship is falling a victim of heartbreak. And the sad news is that, not every relationship you start that will eventually work out as expected. This means that at one point or the other, you will meet with the challenge of coping with a disappointment from the one you love or trusted.

Many who suffer heartbreak especially for the first time, find it hard to successfully scale through. For their lack of knowledge and ability to properly handle situations, some make decisions that bring them even greater pain and continue to be at

9

the losing end while the other partner gets on happily.

For examples, many see the act of disappointment which breaks the heart as an unpardonable offence and consequently, they live with resentment and unforgiveness which further deepens their feelings of hurt. Others develop a general belief from the day they are disappointed that all men or woman are the same (that is, if one person could do it to them, then the other men/women can also do it), and so decide never to truly love again; a decision that keeps them from finding the true love of their life.

Some others take revengeful steps by attempting to hurt the one who has broken their heart; a wrong step that may lead one into going too far and at the end do something regretful. Some others consider the pain of heartbreak unbearable and so take suicidal steps as a way to put a permanent end to their pain, little do they know that a suicidal decision is the worst step one can ever take after a breakup or disappointment because it is the beginning of a more severe pain in hellfire.

Are you a victim of heartbreak? Have you just been told that it is over, by the one your heart deeply goes out to after a long time of being together in a relationship? Are you thinking you have met the worst ever and cannot recover from the shock? If you answered, "Yes" to the above questions, then this book is for you. The purpose of this book is to help you and many others who are facing the same

11

challenge with the strength and courage to successfully cope and move on with life without any feeling of regret.

In this book, you are going to learn what it means to be heartbroken and then the effective steps you need to take to recover from the pain of heartbreak and move on happily with your life.

This Book is therefore a resource material to support you in your journey towards becoming a happy better you, achieving your highest potential and living your best life, especially in the area of love relationship and marriage.

I pray that by the time you're done reading this book, you would have had the strength to happily move on with your life no matter the heartbreak you are currently facing in Jesus' name.

Amen!

Cheers,

Oghovemu Daniel Okpu

PART 1

THE TRUTH ABOUT

HEARTBREAK

THE TRUTH ABOUT HEARTBREAK

By way of introduction, this is the part one of this book, and I will be sharing with you briefly the truth about heartbreak and also my experience with heartbreak.

What is Heartbreak?

Heartbreak is a strong overwhelming emotional, mental or psychological pain we humans experience or feel when we lose or are suddenly abandoned by the person we truly love.

While anyone (family member, friend, etc.) can cause you a heartbreak, most heartbreak experiences are between the opposite sex who are in a strong love (romantic) relationship which they have promised to be fully committed to, no matter the opposing wind that comes to blow them apart. This book focuses on heartbreaks in romantic/love relationships - the emotional pain you feel when the one you have chosen to love unconditionally as a romantic partner suddenly breaks up with you.

Compared to disappointment in other human relationships, the heartbreak in a love or romantic relationship hurts more and so also more difficult to cope with (except you are not a human being). When it happens, it is as though you have made the greatest mistake of your life (the mistake of ever loving at all) from which you will never recover. The cover design of this book illustrates it

16

better. When someone you're emotionally attached to breaks up with you, the heart is torn into parts or pieces hence the experience has been described as heartbreak.

MY ENCOUNTER WITH HEARTBREAK

Briefly, I want to share with you my encounter with heartbreak. Although, I have not really walked through the street of heartbreak, I have crossed the path. Are you confused? Just read on, I will tell you what that means.

Some heartbreaks hurt more than others depending on the length or level of relationship before the breakup. My case was not as deep as such, yet I felt how hurtful it can be when you suddenly discover that you cannot be together with the person your heart truly goes out to, or when such a person all of a sudden decides to drift away from you.

In 2010 or thereabout, when in my final year in the University, I met a lady, Jessy

18

(not her real name) and soon, we became friends. Our friendship grew so fast and strong that we became emotionally attached to each other. As adults, we both understood that we loved ourselves and would make good life partners. Yes, we knew we were in love with each other but then, something happened. Our romantic feelings for each other were not openly (or verbally) expressed so to say.

I will continue but before then, let me say this: Never lie under the blanket of assumption. What do I mean?

Make Your Intention Known Early

Young people make many mistakes that cause them heartbreak. One of these mistakes is the failure to define a relationship early enough. Many men assume that because they love a lady and the lady also loves them, they are automatically into a love relationship with each other. This is not true. As a man, when you have a romantic affection for a lady, and you truly desire her, make your intention known to her in due course, so that she will know where she stands. I have come to realize that, no matter how much love you show to a lady, she takes you as just a friend until you have opened up to her.

So if you are a man, never assume that a lady is already hooked to you until you have made your feelings known to her and not just openly expressing your feelings, she must also be in agreement with you before you can consider her hooked to you.

Without this, she has no blame if she

comes to you tomorrow with her wedding invitation card. And if this happens, you will become heartbroken and you will have yourself to blame, and never the lady.

This was what happened to me. I was the man in the game and it was my responsibility to take the lead – to speak up. For many times, my friend, Jessy tried to use several methods to get out the words she wanted to hear from me but I kept quiet. It never occurred to me that Jessy's conclusion as a lady would be, "It's like, this brother's love for me is on a platonic level, and does not want to have me as a lover." As a matter of fact, this was her mindset, and not to waste her own time or keep others who were on the queue waiting, she resolved to say, 'Yes' to another young man who also loves her and took the step to say to her, "Jessy, I am in love with you."

Jessy truly loved me as a friend so on that platform of friendship, she came visiting one of the days and announced an unexpected news into my ears. With a calm and gentle voice, she said, "Brother Ogho, I want to tell you something and I need you to advise me on what to do." Eager to hear her, I responded, "What is it? Go ahead and tell me." So she started.

"There is this brother who has been on my neck; he loves me and said he wants to marry me." As she spoke on, I was listening to hear how she would end her words. In the end, she said, *"I have finally said 'Yes' to him, and he is ready to do the wedding as soon as possible."*

After she finished speaking, I was calm

and all my responses to her fears or worries concerning her decision didn't show any objection. As she requested, I advised her as a friend and we ended the discussions.

After she had left, I had a cognitive dissonance. I began to feel unusual and uncomfortable as her action was against what I actually wanted. Something in me began to tell me that things were going wrong. To be very sure, I slotted in the cassette of our discussions and replayed the movie-like experience to my wide-opened ears and watched with my clear mental eyes. When I fully realized what was going on; the decision she had taken, the walls of my heart began to crack open. Of course, I felt both disappointed and cheated.

Now, the question is: Why did I feel cheated?

This was my claim: *"Jessy knew that I love and truly love her. Why would she take such a decision without first informing me even though I have not spoken up as she expected."* As a matter of fact, I felt disappointed by her action and was angry. In fact, my heart was broken. This is it! We were never into a certified romantic relationship so to speak, yet, I felt heartbroken. This was what I meant when I said earlier that, *"Although I have not really walked through the street of heartbreak, I have crossed the path."*

Now, if I could feel pain because someone I was emotionally attached to but had not gone into relationship with

24

was leaving me, how much more hurt or heartbroken will you feel if someone who has already promised to marry you suddenly says he/she is no more interested in the relationship and disappears from your life?

So, what is the truth about heartbreak I want you to know here? It is simply the fact that, it's indeed a terrible, painful and devastating experience.

That said, there is however a good news for you. You must have heard the quote that, *"Life is 10% what happens to you and 90% your reaction to what happens to you,"* and this is what it means:

When something happens to you, what you eventually become ("happy and better" or "bitter and worse"), is majorly

25

the result of your reaction or response towards the event and not actually the event itself. Yes, a person remains a failure not mainly because of what happens to him/her, but because of his/her attitude towards what happens.

Someone has said, **"Don't cry because it is over. Smile because it happened."** In other words, when you have a relationship or marriage breakup, face the experience with a positive mindset (smile that it happened), instead of reacting negatively to it (crying because it is over). If you must cry at all, it shouldn't be because you feel it is over, but because it is necessary to release your hurtful feeling so you can move on.

Now here is the good news I've got for you. While a heartbreak experience may

26

really be painful and devastating, handling it with the right or positive attitude turns it into a stepping stone that takes one to a greater height. No matter how painful a disappointment appears to be, taking the right steps turns the pain into gain. In other words, a person only continues to suffer the life draining effects of a heartbreak challenge when the experience is considered as a misfortune instead of taking it as just an experience of life, and approached it from that negative angle.

It was in this light M. Kathleen Casey said, ***"Pain is inevitable, suffering is optional."*** Meaning that, although you can't totally avoid the hurtful feeling or pain caused by a breakup (because you are human), you can choose not to let it eat you up or place your life on hold.

How can you handle a heartbreak experience and not be negatively affected or allow it to stop you from enjoying your best life?

The answer to the above question is the crux of this book. Let's now get on to the next part where I will share with you 21 helpful steps (or strategies) to cope with heartbreak, recover from its pain, and happily move on to live your best life.

PART 2

STEPS TO HEALING YOUR BROKEN HEART

21 Proven Steps To Cope With Heartbreak, Recover From Its Pain, And Happily Move On With Your Life

As I shared in part 1, from personal experience, facing a disappointment in a romantic relationship you believed would end in a desired destination or lasting marriage is indeed heartbreaking. But when it happens, don't let it destroy you or stop you from enjoying the rest of your life. Taking the steps I'm about to share in this part 2 will help you to carefully handle your broken heart, recover the pieces to form a whole healthy heart again, and happily move on to live your best life.

I strongly believe that by the time you are done reading these 21 steps, you would have got what it takes to cope with a relationship disappointment or breakup, recover from its pain and move on with your life without having anything to lose or regret, but be grateful that it made you become a happy better you.

However, just before I walk you through these steps, let me say this as it is very important. It's not every step that may be applicable to every situation and everyone. While some may be applied in all situations and by anyone, others are only applicable to certain situations and the individual involved for expected positive result.

Let's now begin.

STEP #1

Accept The Reality

It has been said that, *"Acceptance is an important part of healing after a breakup. This is the first step that will help you move on."*

Jude suddenly broke up with Kate and it took Kate weeks to believe it. When Jude was already far gone, Kate was still thinking that it was a dream and not a reality. Although she was feeling the absence of Jude, she would not accept it that it was real. In the midst of her pain, she kept hoping that Jude would return. The more she waited, the farther Jude disappears and the deeper the cuts in her heart.

By the time she finally came to her senses that Jude was actually gone, she had suffered so much. And not until she believed the reality, she continued to wallow in pain.

Dear reader, though that is an imaginary case, it does happen in reality. When you meet with a breakup with the one your heart loves, don't pretend and act as if nothing happened when truly something did happen. In the event of a heartbreak, do not lie to yourself or others that nothing is wrong. Accept the reality and believe it. Accepting the reality is vital because it is after you have come to terms with the reality that a healing process begins.

STEP #2

Let The Tears Flow

To get over the pain of heartbreak, you need to express your emotions; how you feel. This is important because, venting your emotions reduces the pressure of the hurtful feelings in you.

One way to express your hurtful feeling is to let the tears flow when they need to. Some people think or believe that it is wrong to cry. Crying is not a wrong thing to do in as much as you don't act like a baby when crying. A baby cannot control himself when crying and can do it any where and any time without minding who is watching. This is not what I'm recommending here because it is totally wrong to act this way.

First, crying is a sign of true love for someone or something. When you lose someone or something very dear to you and your mood does not show it, your claim of love can be said to be in doubt. As a matter of fact, you may be considered a pretender.

The shortest verse in the Bible is John 11:35 and it reads, *"Jesus wept."* Now, imagine the Lord of Host, who has the power to do all things shedding tears because his dear friend, Lazarus was dead. Why do you think Jesus cried? Jesus wept not because he lacked the power to bring Lazarus back to life. No. He is all-powerful and he eventually raised him back to life. He cried to

35

express his feelings as a human being. When he saw Lazarus' two sisters, Mary and Martha together with the rest people helplessly weeping, he could not suppress his own feelings too. The best he could do was to let it out by simply allowing the tears to flow.

It has been scientifically proven that a person feels better about a hurting situation after shedding tears. So when you meet with a heartbreak and you are deeply hurt, let the tears freely flow when you can't hold it back anymore. Doing this helps to release the emotional pain welling up in you and once the tears flow out, you feel better.

In addition to crying, another way humans express or release pain is to feel sad. When you are heartbroken, give yourself time to be in a quiet mood.

However, while you express your pain through crying or being in a sad state, here is something very important you must bear in mind. Know when to say it is time to stop crying or feeling sad. Put in different words, you must never allow your emotions to control you. Instead, you should be in charge of your feelings. You are in control of your emotions when you are able to put yourself together and do what needs to be done no matter the pain you may be feeling.

Yes, that it is necessary to cry or express your sad feelings does not mean that you should act like a baby as already mentioned, or spend weeks shedding tears and feeling depressed. No. When you fail to control your feelings and quit

37

being sad at the right time, you start to cause harm to yourself and life in general.

STEP #3

Connect With Loved Ones

No matter the mistakes you made that might have brought a breakup, or how much people hate you, there are those who still care about you. These people accept you just as you are. They want to see you happy and so are ready to stand by you in times of challenges. These are your loved ones.

During dark moments or period of pains, loved ones such as family members and friends are a good source of strength and encouragement. When your heart is broken, and you desire healing, spend time with people who love you in spite of your flaws. Share your feelings with

39

them; tell them how heartbroken you feel; tell them your worries and fears and their words of advice and encouragement will give you hope and make you feel better.

It's true that they may not be able to bring back to you that partner who drifted away, but their words, feeling of warmness, listening ears, and love, will help and give you comfort. The feeling or thought that they love and care for you will remind you of the fact that you are not a good-for-nothing or worthless person that people think you are. The more you spent time with those who love and care about you, the more the broken pieces of your heart gather together and get healed up

This strategy or step greatly helped me

40

during my period of heartbreak. When I felt heartbroken as I narrated in part 1 of this book, words of encouragement from family members and friends helped to heal my bleeding wounds faster. Try this yourself and see the wonder it does.

Let me mention this before we move on to the next step. The first and best person to connect with during heartbreak before friends and relatives is your Creator, God Almighty. You will see more on this in step 20.

41

STEP #4

Don't Blame Yourself

If you are going through a heartbreak challenge, do not beat yourself up. Don't blame or run yourself down. Casting blames on yourself makes you feel sorry for yourself and the more you live in self-pity, the greater the pain you experience and the longer it lasts.

One truth about life I have come to know is that, a person will not always get what he wants at a particular time he actually wants it. Yes; sometimes, people don't get what they want no matter how much they strive for it. Accepting this truth will help you a lot.

Jess Rothenberg once said, **_"You can obsess and obsess over how things ended – what you did wrong or could have done differently – but there's not much of a point. It's not like it'll change anything. So really, why worry?"_**

There is a great lesson to learn from Jess' statement, and the lesson is that, no matter how much you blame yourself or worry over a relationship or marriage breakup, it will not change what has happened. Saying, "I caused it, I would have done this or that" or focusing too much on what you did or what you should have done that you didn't do won't change the state of things.

There is no point blaming yourself

because, even if it is actually your fault, or you caused the whole situation, there is nothing you can do about it to change the situation. Who left has already gone. So if you can't change things, what then is the need of regretting and blaming yourself?

Never worry over a relationship that ended. If it was good, then that is wonderful. If it was bad, then you have experience. All you need to do is to learn the lessons from your experience so that you don't repeat them in your next relationship.

STEP #5

Stop Thinking You Are At The Losing End

You will hardly get over a heartbreak experience if you think that you have lost something. Rather than feeling, "Hey, I have missed John, a very rich, nice, caring guy," say to yourself, "John has missed a virtuous woman, the type of lady that is hard to see."

Note; this will only work if indeed you're a virtuous lady. So you must always strive to be one. This applies to both parties.

With this mindset that you're not at the losing end, you will not feel rejected. You

45

won't feel you are unworthy or not good enough. This makes you feel relieved and relaxed. But if you are of the feeling that "I will miss John, it will be hard to find his cool, caring and nice nature," you will become more hurt and heartbroken.

To easily move on from your state of heartbreak, see him/her as the person who loses and not you. Say to yourself using the words of R. H. Sin, *"I did not lose you; you lost me. You will search for me inside of everyone you're with and I won't be found."*

To see yourself as one who never loses and recover faster, believe in yourself. Be proud of who you are. See yourself as a treasure that the one who left you is losing. Never feel worthless because of a relationship that is breaking up (or has

46

already broken up). When feeling rejected, remind yourself of the great treasure you carry. Don't sit dejectedly wondering if you will ever be enough for anyone. Instead, say to yourself, "I'm enough and will always be enough. I know that when my time comes, I will meet someone who will value me and appreciate the treasure I'm."

Janet (not her real name) who once suffered heartbreak said, "I always speak to myself before the mirror positive things like, 'I'm beautiful, I have fine set of teeth, beautiful nose and face...' and touching my cheeks, I would find my self smiling and admiring myself that I'm beautifully made and that I love myself." She further said, "I went into dressing and adorning myself gorgeously with the little clothings I had."

Just like Janet, love yourself. Accept who you are even when others reject or tag you a "not-good-enough" to have. Don't look tattered. Instead, dress well and look smart believing that you're good, and who left you has missed a great treasure. With this mindset, you feel better and your broken heart heals up faster.

STEP #6

Avoid Contact/Stop Communication

Let me reveal this truth to you. In a love relationship, you are emotionally bonded or connected to your partner, and this bond was formed as a result of your consistent contact and communication with each other.

When there is a relationship breakup, this bond experiences what I call, a **'stretching'** and it is this stretching that produces heartbreak or an emotional breakdown. To heal this heartbreak, the bond has to be slacked and finally separated, and the only way to loose this emotional attachment is to avoid contact

49

and communication. Remember, consistent contact and communication was what formed the bond. In the same way, to break the bond between you and the one who has chosen to leave you, you have to avoid contact and communication with each other.

If you are currently experiencing heartbreak, and you desire to heal your heart wounds faster, cut off every possible means of interacting or communicating with your partner. As already said, this is important so that you can break the bond that exists between the both of you. Until this emotional attachment is disconnected, you will keep experiencing pain as a result of the 'stretching' that occurs due to his/her departure.

How do you avoid him/her? Get rid of anything that can tempt you to want to reach out to him/her. E.g, phone numbers, avoid places you know you're likely to meet or see him/her. For instance, on social media platforms such as Facebook, etc.; but if you can't totally stay away from social media, then block him/her so that you can't see or contact each other.

What more should you do to break the emotional bond? For the meantime, stay away from the things that bring his/her memory. E.g. the pictures you took together, the games you both enjoyed playing together, the places or joints where you both sat and had discussions, friends that always talk about him/her, etc. This is to gradually remove or kill the romantic memory, love or feelings you
51

have for him/her.

However, note that there are exceptions. Avoiding someone who has broken your heart never means you should stop church meetings if you both worship in the same church. And of course, you can't resign from work just because you want to stop seeing a colleague who betrayed or disappointed you.

Now, the question is, what should you do when situations force you to contact or meet with the one who has broken up with you? Remember step 1. Accept the reality that both of you are no more partners as far as love relationship is concern. Also, remember step 5. Never feel you are at the losing end. Each time you see him/her, tell yourself, "He/she missed me. I wish he/she knew this..." I hope you got the point clearly.

This step will not be complete if I do not say this.

As already inferred, avoiding the one who broke up with you is never to keep enmity. Instead, your avoidance of him/her is to help kill the romantic feelings you have for him/her. The fact that you are no more romantic lovers does not mean you cannot relate or even be friends. To let you know, Jessy and I are still friends till date.

In a nutshell, avoiding your ex-partner may not be a forever decision. But remember, your bond of friendship should never be as strong as it was before the breakup or before you started relationship, especially when one partner is already married.

53

To conclude, I want you to bear in mind this quote by an anonymous. He said, **"Sometimes you have to forget what you want in order to remember what you deserve. Anybody that chooses to leave you does not deserve your love. Therefore, if you must remember the one that truly deserves your love, then you must forget the one that does not deserve it even though you still want him/her."**

STEP #7

Never Feel Pitied Or Sorrowful Before Him/Her

When you have a breakup with your partner, you may think or feel that it's because you are not worthy or good enough. See, even if he/she told you to your face that you are not good enough, and that is the reason he/she cannot remain with you, never accept or believe it. Never allow that thought to settle in your heart and begin to pity or feel sorry for yourself.

If the one you truly love decides to leave you because he/she says you are not good enough, let him or her go away. You don't even need a person who cannot accept you for who you are. Anyone who looks down on you does not deserve your love. So when he/she chooses to leave, remain proud of your identity; who you are. Be confident of yourself and maintain a healthy self-esteem.

As shown in the preceding step, you cannot always avoid seeing the one who has disappointed you. So, whenever you cross paths with this person, never feel pitied or look sorrowful before him/her. In other words, do not feel shame or embarrassed. Feeling shame or pitied raises his/her ego. Instead of feeling shame that you were rejected or jilted, be happy and wear a bright countenance.

Rather than feeling disappointed, be proud that you have the boldness to tell someone that, "I love you" because not everybody does this for fear of rejection. You took the risk only that it did not work out as you desired. And who has not failed before? Now, you have learned great lessons which those who never tried do not know.

The importance of maintaining a healthy self-esteem or self-confidence during a relationship heartbreak cannot be over-emphasized. If you don't maintain a high self-esteem and you allow self-pity to eat into you, you will continue to feel hurt. Your heart wounds will continue to bleed until your heart is totally destroyed. This happens when you can no longer move on to do the things that matter to the fulfillment of God's purpose for your life.

STEP #8

Be Busy Doing What You Love

As J. C. Ryle quoted, *"Idleness is the devil's best friend. It is the surest way to give him an opportunity of doing us some harm. An idle mind is like an open door, and if Satan does not come through it himself, it is certain he will throw something in to arouse bad thoughts in us."*

The above expression by J. C Ryle could not have been said in a better way. For real, staying idle and bemoaning what has happened to you is giving the devil opportunity to carry out his evil works in you.

When you are idle, you think about how you have been badly treated by the one you truly love. And if this continues, the devil might suggest to you some ways you can smite or get back at the person who left you. And you know, doing anything funny will worsen the situation.

So to prevent this, keep yourself busy with those activities that you love when you are experiencing heartbreak. What are the things you love? These could be household chores, reading, singing hymns/songs and meditating on God's word, watching healthy movies, playing games, and the like.

Do you love teaching? Look for an opportunity to impact what you know into others. Do you love helping others? Forget your own pain and go look for

59

someone who might need you to put a smile on his or her face.

Do you have passion for storytelling? Look for an audience to share your story with. You can even choose to do this with your social media friends. Rather than allowing the thought of your heartbreak to break you down and make you become depressed, pick up activities that make you feel happy and fulfilled. As you continue to do this, gradually, your heart pain is going away and before you know it, you have become totally healed.

STEP #9

Turn Your Experience Into Art

One sure way to cope with heartbreak and recover faster is to turn your experience into art. In the words of Shane L. Koyczan, *"If your heart is broken, make art with the pieces."*

For Jordan Bates, it was writing. Hear his words:

"After she told me the bad news, I felt an eruption of emotion that was unlike anything I've ever felt. There was just so much of it. I needed to let it out somehow, so I wrote."

He continued, *"Writing was a rock, something that had been there*

61

before and was still there, something I could turn to. I wrote poetry and letters and stories. Translating experience into art was a type of catharsis. It was a way to channel the energies, to release them, to cleanse myself."

What form of art can you make from the broken pieces of your heart? Yours may not be writing. It can be dancing, painting, singing or whatever. Doing this will help you in your recovering process.

STEP #10

Create Time For Exercise

Do you know that physical exercise causes the human body to release a happiness chemical called serotonin? When serotonin is released during a physical exercise, you begin to feel happy. Several studies have shown that exercise improves a person's mood and increases self-confidence or self-esteem.

If you are experiencing heartbreak, exercise will help you overcome the challenge by improving your mood or state of happiness. You don't have to do a full workout. Anything like taking a 10-15 minutes' daily walk, going to the gym or the swimming pool (knowing that you

63

can swim), jugging, running, or any other physical activity that makes you sweat is enough to put your mind into proper shape.

Whenever you're feeling hurt or downcast as a result of a breakup, get up from your bed of self-pity, regret, depression, sorrow and pain, and engage your body in a physical activity that makes you sweat and causes your heart to beat faster.

STEP #11

Laugh Out Your Blue Feeling

Earlier on, I told you that, 'crying' is a step that can help you to get over your feeling of heartbreak. Yes, it is if done in the right way. In the same manner, laughter is a proven recovery pill for a broken heart. Just as cry can help you to recover from the pain of heartbreak, laughter is a great antidote for reducing the painful feeling that is caused by a relationship breakup.

As a matter of fact, what a healing balm is to a bruised flesh, so is laughter to a heart that is emotionally broken. So whenever you see yourself turning blue (feeling sad), use the rod of laughter to

65

beat yourself until you start weeping. I hope you understand this.

Does this mean you should keep laughing for no reason? Not at all. Or else, you will be considered an insane person. So how do you induce laughter when you don't' feel like it?

Look for anything that can induce it.

Here are some things you can do to make you laugh even when you don't want to.

- ✓ Watch and listen to healthy comedy shows.
- ✓ Play with little children.
- ✓ Visit that your jovial friend that always makes you laugh, etc.

The period of time you engage in these stuffs that make you laugh, you experience a great sense of relief and happiness as you tend to forget what had happen. And as you keep doing this, your heart wounds are getting healed up gradually.

STEP #12

Travel To A New World

Have you ever had a change of environment before? If yes, how did you feel in your new place compared to your previous environment? Better of course.

Yes, it has been proven that a change of environment brings new feelings and mindset about life. For this reason, changing environment can serve as a great medicine to an emotionally wounded heart. Indeed, being in an entirely different environment after a relationship breakup goes a long way to helping you recover from the pain. This is because in a new environment, you meet new people, make new friends, visit new

68

places, and have new experiences, and all of these take your mind entirely from what has happened to you.

Although this step is very effective, one may not be able to take it for some factors beyond control. Some of these factors include: Lack of finance to foot travelling bills, job and family responsibilities, etc. So, if travelling to a new place is not possible due to any of these mentioned factors or anything else that you can't control, then do it on the wings of media. Resting on the wings of media, you can travel round the world if not the universe and experience new things.

What do I mean by wings of media? By this, I simply mean changing your environment through books and movies.

Are you heartbroken? Get some fictional books and movies to read and watch. This definitely takes you mentally away to another world where you meet with new people and experience new things. While you are away meeting new people and experiencing new things, the scattered pieces of your heart gradually come together forming a whole healthy heart that makes you have a new and better perspective about life.

STEP #13

Look For Someone Else To Help

Have you been in a situation where you helped someone going through tough time and in the process you forgot your own problem? If you've not, try it out and see how great it works.

To help you recover from your heartbroken state faster than you imagine, look for a person who is going through a heartbreak experience as you are or other similar experiences and give the help or encouragement you can. In the process of doing this, it will surprise you how fast your wounded heart gets healed up.

71

One way to do this is to turn your seemingly mess into a message and preach this message to others. Share your own pain with them and let them know that they are not alone in the race of heartbreak experience. Tell them the lessons you have learnt from your own heartbreak experience; the strategies you are employing to get over your heart pain and how they can also apply the same in their own life.

Give them hope that heartbreak experience is not the end of life, but just an experience at one point or the other in the journey of life.

Helping others can also be in other areas. What strengths do you have that you can use to make others happy and make life easier for them? Use it. Give to the

72

needy; look for someone to cloth and feed, visit the sick, help someone do a difficult task; show someone how to do something.

As you take your time to do these, you will hardly have time to think about your pain, and when your mind is on positive things, the healing process is quickened up.

STEP #14

Don't Compare Yourself With Others

Comparing your relationship with that of others (such as friends, colleagues, family members, etc.) is one worse thing you can do to yourself when you are facing the pain of a relationship breakup. Don't do this because it is destructive; it deepens the cuts in your heart.

Never say, "Look at Mary enjoying a beautiful relationship with her partner. See John with his beautiful partner already planning marriage, and here I'm, facing one disappointment after the other." No, it's bad to do this.

You should realize that everyone faces

one challenge or the other in life. You can't tell what those you are comparing yourself to now may be facing in their own life. You can't tell what the next minute holds for them.

If you are comparing your life with others, and thinking they are better than you because of their relationship or marriage that is working, you are only using one area of life to judge the whole. Don't use one aspect of life to give verdict on the whole because your verdict will be wrong. Yes, they may truly be enjoying a great relationship or marriage, but do you know the pain they may be facing in other areas of their life? To them, you may even be better off; wishing they are enjoying life as you.

So, to recover from the pain of your

75

broken heart, remove eyes from the life of others. If you must look at them, let it be for a healthy reason. Maybe to learn from them; what they may be doing which you can apply in your life to also enjoy the type of relationship/marriage they are having. Instead of letting the thought of their beautiful relationship break you down, let it inspire and build you up by learning the strategies that are working for them.

STEP #15

Recover Fully Before Loving Again

After a breakup, while some take too long time to love again for fear of getting heartbroken the second time, others are too much in a hurry to start another relationship. One thing that people do that makes them suffer constant heartbreak is rushing into another relationship too soon after a breakup. They do this because they think that getting into another relationship will help to fill up their empty heart. They believe that by doing this, they won't miss the perks or moments of happiness they had in the broken relationship.

Dear reader, don't rush into a new relationship just after a breakup when you are yet to get over your emotional pain. Take time to heal up first before thinking of giving your heart to another person to occupy. Now, you may want to ask why I'm saying this, and I will tell you the reason.

A person who is experiencing heartbreak is like someone under the influence of anger. Have you heard the saying that, ***"When you are angry, do not take any serious decision?"*** If yes, why do you think this advice is given?

It is wise to take no serious decision in anger because, in a state of anger, the mind is not in its proper frame. Any decision made in that state is most likely to be wrong. This is why many regret the actions they took in anger after their minds have calm down.

This also applies to heartbreak. When you are heartbroken, especially at the early stage, you are under what I call a psychological or emotional trauma, which is a state where your mind or thinking faculty is distorted as a result of the hurting feeling. In this state of mind, you think abnormally so to speak. Your eyes and ears see and hear double.

Consequently, anyone you see or that comes your way at this point appears to be a godsend; a perfect partner that comes to mend your broken heart, and in a bid to fill up your emptiness, you start a fresh relationship immediately. But just after some weeks into your new found love, you discover that this person is not a godsend as you initially thought.

Now tell me, how will you feel when you realize that the relationship you rushed into is a wrong one? Of course, you will become more heartbroken; your already existing heart wounds yet to be healed up will cut even deeper. And you know, the deeper and wider the cuts, the longer the time it takes the broken heart to heal up and become whole again.

So, to recover faster from your broken heart and move on happily with your life, you should not ignore this step. Don't go into a relationship immediately after a breakup. Give yourself time to fully recover before you love again.

STEP #16

Avoid Making Big Decisions

Apart from the decision of rushing into another relationship, there are other big decisions you should avoid making when you have not recovered from a heartbreak.

Yes, taking big decisions during the season of heartbreak may lead to more heartbreaks. This is because you might be under the influence of your hurting heart. It is like taking decisions in a state of anger, and you know what that means as I just explained in the preceding step. Like anger, the emotions are high or strong during a heartbreak. Your mind is not in its proper frame. So there is every tendency to decide wrongly.

So, what are some of these big decisions you should not make when facing the challenge of heartbreak?

Here are some examples:

Changing your job, relocating to a new city, changing your school or taking up a new course, etc. Taking any of these decisions requires that you actually know the implications of what you want to do. In a broken state, it's difficult for the heart to think properly and take things in the right perspective. So, to avoid making mistakes that you will later regret when your eyes are clear, wisdom teaches that you wait a little moment after a breakup before concluding on taking a major decision in your life.

82

For example, let's say your ex-partner works with you in the same company. You might be tempted to resign just to stop seeing him/her. This is a major decision, and it's foolish to take it. Why should you resign from your job, your source of income just because someone broke your heart? When you take such a decision under the influence of heartbreak, you will regret it later by the time you begin to face financial difficulty.

However, there are situations where it might be necessary to take a major decision. E.g, relocating to another city as discussed in step 12 (Travelling to a new world). In as much as doing this does not have any negative implication, you can take it. Remember I mentioned at the beginning of this part 2 that, not every step is applicable in every situation or to everyone. Therefore, know when and where a step is applicable or necessary and take it.

STEP #17

Realize That Others Have Also Suffered The Same Thing

"When my girlfriend dumped me, I turned to the Internet to read about break-ups. What I found were countless stories of people who had suffered precisely what I had. Reading those stories was therapeutic because I no longer felt so helpless or worthless. I felt connected to the billions of other people who'd felt equally awful. I gained respect for my ancestors and my contemporaries, for the strength of the human race. I started to have faith that I too could find the

85

resilience to survive and reconstruct my world," wrote Jordan Bates

See, no matter what we pass through in life, there were people who had gone through similar cases in the past, and there are others who are presently going through that or similar pain. So, what does that tell you? It simply means that you are not the first to be disappointed in a relationship. The question you should ask is how those who were once victims survived it?

To get answer, connect with them, read their experiences and how they were able to overcome and happily move on with your life. This was what Jordan Bates did and you can see his testimony above. Like Jordan, I assure you, after hearing others' stories of heartbreak or breakup, you will realize that yours is a little one compared to theirs, and if they could scale through unscathed, then you can also. This awareness gives you strength and courage to move on with your life.

In a nutshell, realizing that you are not alone in the race of heartbreak and hearing others' victory over the challenge of heartbreak will encourage and help you get back up from the bed of regret, sadness, depression, hopelessness and heart pain.

STEP # 18

See The Benefits The Breakup Offers

Building a relationship with someone means a lot of things. One of those things is the fact that you have to make some adjustments to your lifestyle. For examples, creating time for your partner, making financial commitment, giving up some activities or wears you love just because you want to please the one you love.

The very moment this special person leaves your life, you no more have the constraint to do those things that were not part of you, but only chose to do them to get along with your partner.

88

After a breakup, you're no more under obligation to sacrifice your time, income and other resources to stay committed to your partner.

When a breakup occurs and you feel heartbroken, think of these benefits you stand to gain. Now, you don't have to spend money on anyone; you now have enough time for yourself; you can now wear those heeled shoes you abandoned because of him; you can now keep those beards you love which she never liked, etc.

So, instead of feeling heartbroken and thinking that life has ended because of one human being that chose to leave you, think of the many great things you stand to enjoy and the opportunity to build a better relationship.

Note that...

Going back to the things you once enjoyed never include the bad habits or negative lifestyle you were living. If your ex-partner made some positive changes in you, keep to the changes and do not go back to the former even though the partner is no more in your life. I can say that he/she entered your life to help you make those positive changes and then leave so that you can attract your true life partner.

Just before I take you to the next step, I want you to note something very important. It's not every relationship that is meant to end in marriage. I can say that some relationships are only meant to help you develop those characters and

90

have the experiences you need to build a relationship with the right person who will become your life or marriage partner. So, after that partner has fulfilled his or her purpose of coming into your life, he or she has to go so that the right life partner can find you.

Having made this clear to you, let's now move on to the next step.

STEP #19

Share Your Ordeal With Wisdom

In step #3, I shared the importance of connecting with loved ones (Family members and friends). Yes, sharing your heart pain with people eases your pain. No doubt about that, but there is something very vital you must bear in mind while you open up your painful experiences to people.

What is it?

It's not everyone who wants your happiness or success. This is a gospel truth of life that is worth knowing. Many people (including so-called family members and friends) you think that love

92

you never do. It is for this reason Scripture says that a man's enemies are members of his own household (See Matt. 10:36, Micah 7:6). Yes, there are many who claim to love you but are jealous of you and are looking for an opportunity to ridicule you.

Moreso, some persons are not just mature or trustworthy enough to confide in and these include relatives and friends. When you tell them some personal issues, they will handle things in an immature way though it may not be their intention to hurt you.

For instance, these persons may not use your story against you, but they may not be able to keep it from people who might use it against you. Or would you want to hear people you never expect, discussing your issues in a manner and on platforms you never imagine? I believe you wouldn't as this can cause you more emotional pain.

In view of the above, carefully choose those you discuss your relationship (and other sensitive personal) issues with. I know you may want to release your painful feelings by sharing how you feel with relatives and friends, but know that not every family member or friend deserves to hear your painful story.

So taking the step to be selective in the choice of those you confide in is very vital to the recovery process of your broken heart.

STEP #20

Connect With The One Whose Love Never Fails

"Listen to God with a broken heart. He is not only the doctor who mends it but also the father who wipes away the tears," said Criss Jami

See, no matter how much a person claims to love you today, a time will come when that person will turn his or her heart away from you. If you don't know this before, know it now. In life, people claim to love you when things are well with you. But when it's the opposite, the love reduces and finally fails. Hence the rate of heartbreak tends to increase.

You met a man or lady today and you are overwhelmed with his/her promises to love you forever. Some can even go as far as saying they will die for you. But with just a little wind of challenge that comes your way, you see this same person who promised to stick with you no matter what comes, going away without an iota of concern for you. That is human being for you.

But do you know that there is someone whose love for you never fails? Regardless of who you're, your mistakes, your imperfections and faults, His love is constant and eternal. In other words, He loves you unconditionally forever.

Who is this person?

He is no other person but the one who formed you; your Creator. According to the Scriptures, He said, **"I have loved you with an everlasting love; I have drawn you with unfailing kindness."** Jer. 31:3.

In season when human's love fails, God's love for you remains. His big Hands are wide open to draw you to Himself with an unfailing kindness. So when human beings forsake you and you are down, feeling disappointed and heartbroken, turn to God whose love for you does not fail.

Pour your heart pains to Him. Tell Him how bad you feel and ask Him to heal your broken heart. As you fellowship with Him, trust me, you will begin to feel His comforting Hands patting your back. You will hear Him saying to you, "Son/daughter, don't worry, even if everyone abandons you, I will never leave you." Believe me, as you keep hearing His comforting voice, your wounds will begin to heal up.

I can keep taking you through more steps but I wish to end the list. However, there is a step I cannot leave out on this list. It's so important that, applying all of the above 20 steps is useless (they will yield no positive result) if I do not share this particular one with you.

What is it?

It is the step of forgiveness. Now, let's get on to the next page to fully discuss it.

STEP #21

Take The Bold Step Of Forgiveness

Hardly can we see a broken relationship where one partner is not offended. Yes, when the breakup is not mutually agreed on by the two parties involved, one of them is usually offended, and because of the hurt caused, it is usually hard to forgive.

In my counselling sessions with victims of heartbreak who find it hard to move on, I discovered that one of their problems is the difficulty to forgive the person who broke their heart. Considering the degree of the pain caused, they continue to hate and resent their offender.

99

Dear reader, do you still find it hard to forgive? Is there an ex-partner that you still keep in the prison of your heart because you felt maltreated? Then, it may be hard for you to fully recover from your pain and happily move on with your life. But I believe that you paid for this book and you're taking your time to read it because you really want to recover from your heartbreak experience.

It was C. Joybell C. who quoted, *"If you want to forget something or someone, never hate it, or never hate him/her. Everything and everyone that you hate is engraved upon your heart; if you want to let go of something, if you want to forget, you cannot hate."*

Joybell has almost said it all. As I

mentioned in the preceding step, none of the strategies I have discussed in this book for coping with a heartbreak or disappointment challenge will yield positive result if you do not take the bold step to forgive the one who broke your heart or disappointed you.

You're finding it hard to forgive because you claim that he/she disappointed you after promising you marriage. I want you to realize an important truth. Although I have mentioned it before somewhere in this book, I want to repeat it so it can sink deeply into your subconscious mind. It's not every relationship that is meant to end in marriage.

Some relationships are only meant to help you learn and grow into a happy better version of yourself that can better handle the challenges that come with marriage. So for you to attract the right person, that relationship has to break up. I believe you are getting the point I am making here.

The importance of forgiveness in healing your broken heart cannot be overemphasized. Knowing the beauty of forgiveness after experiencing a heartbreak, Lailah Gifty Akita said, *"Forgiveness heals any brokenness in the heart."* This is just the hard truth. The one who refuses to forgive an offender, suffers more pain than the offender. Let me repeat that to you. The one who refuses to forgive an offender, suffers more pain than the offender. Did you get it? This is because, your anger, grudges and resentment against your offender are like thorns that keep piecing your wounded heart, increasing the pain and making it to bleed even more severely.

Do you remember that we are all offenders before God? Can you say that for the past 24 hours, you have not offended God?

Just before I wrap up this last and most important step, let me quickly draw your mind to what Jesus Christ said about forgiveness. Quoting Him from the Bible book of Matthew 6:14-15 (Amplified Version), He said,

"*For if you forgive people their trespasses [their reckless and willful sins, leaving them, letting them go, and giving up resentment], your heavenly Father will also forgive you. But if you do not forgive others their trespasses [their reckless and willful sins, leaving them, letting them go, and giving up resentment], neither will your heavenly Father forgive you."*

See, I do not try to ignore the fact that some offences are hard to forgive. Infact, some appear to be unforgivable especially when the relationship has caused you some irreparable mistakes such as losing your virginity, killing of your unborn innocent baby on the table of abortion, contracting an incurable disease, etc.

But then, refusing to forgive no matter how great the offence may be will keep your heart perpetually broken and not only that, your relationship with God will be negatively affected. Yes, you can't freely connect with Him because of your sins that will not also be forgiven (Matt. 6:15), a state that keeps you from enjoying your life.

So with this, if you truly want to be healed of your broken heart, find better love and enjoy a more fulfilling relationship/marriage, forgiving your offender is a must.

Wait; have I mentioned to you in this book that you are a potential carrier? That is the name I call my readers. Yes, you carry in you the ability to become a happy better version of yourself, unleash your potentials and live your best life.

Don't say you can't forgive because one of the potentials God has given to us is
105

the ability to forgive others. Yes, otherwise Jesus Christ would not have asked us to forgive our offenders. Who needs your forgiveness? To ensure your broken heart is healed, you have to release your ability to forgive.

No matter the pain the one who broke your heart has caused you, decide today, and say, "I forgive him/her!" It may be painful to do, but trust me, you will allow your bleeding heart to heal faster as there will be no more thorns of anger and resentment to choke it.

Even if he/she does not feel guilty and beg for forgiveness, forgive all the same just as God forgives us unconditionally. If you can take this last and most important step, alongside the others, you will recover from your heartbreak and move

106

on   to   live   your   best   life.

PART 3

30 PROFOUND QUOTES

ON HEARTBREAK

30 Profound Quotes On Heartbreak That Will Quicken Your Healing Process

1. I hate to say it, most of them are going to break your heart, but you can't give up because if you give up, you'll never find your soulmate. You'll never find that half who makes you whole and that goes for everything. Just because you fail once, doesn't mean you're gonna fail at everything. Keep trying, hold on, and always, always, always believe in yourself, because if you don't, then who will? So keep your head high, keep your chin up, and most importantly, keep smiling, because life's a beautiful thing and there's so

much to smile about. **Marilyn Monroe**

2. Sometimes, it takes a heartbreak to shake us awake and help us see we are worth so much more than we're settling for. **Mandy Hale**

3. Sometimes we must undergo hardships, breakups, and narcissistic wounds, which shatter the flattering image that we had of ourselves, in order to discover two truths: that we are not who we thought we were; and that the loss of a cherished pleasure is not necessarily the loss of true happiness and well-being. **Jean-Yves Leloup**

4. Getting over a painful experience is much like crossing monkey bars. You have to let go at some points in order to move forward. **C.S. Lewis**

5. Blessed are those with cracks in their broken heart because that is how the light gets in. **Shannon L. Alder**

6. And anything that might hurt me would just make me stronger in the end. **Elizabeth Eulberg**

7. Relationships are like broken glass. Sometimes it's better to leave them broken than hurt yourself trying to put the pieces back together. **Alex Haditaghi**

8. Birds sing even when the world is filled with sadness. I don't know why people can't do the same thing. **Michael Gilbert**

9. Love can stretch you beyond what you feel you can endure. But you can, and you must get back to love and living! **–Staci A. Welch-Bartley**

10. It is our wounds that create in us a desire to reach for miracles. The fulfillment of such miracles depends on whether we let our wounds pull us down or lift us up towards our dreams. **Jocelyn Soriano**

11. You can obsess and obsess over how things ended – what you did wrong or could have done differently – but

there's not much of a point. It's not like it'll change anything. So really, why worry? **Jess Rothenberg**

12. When things are falling apart, know they are actually falling into place. **Staci A. Welch-Bartley**

13. One of the best times for figuring out who you are and what you really want out of life is right after a breakup. **Mandy Hale**

14. No matter how bad you want a person, if your hearts are in two different places, you'll have to pass and move on. **Alexandra Elle**

15. Hearts can break. Yes, hearts can break. Sometimes, I think it would

be better if we died when they did, but we don't. **Stephen King**

16. Someday, you're going to look back on this moment of your life as such a sweet time of grieving. You'll see that you were in mourning and your heart was broken, but your life was changing... **Elizabeth Gilbert**

17. If your heart is broken, make art with the pieces. **Shane L. Koyczan**

18. Forgiveness heals any brokenness in the heart. **Lailah Gifty Akita**

19. Listen to God with a broken heart. He is not only the doctor who mends it but also the father who wipes away the tears. **Criss Jami**

20. To be rejected by someone doesn't mean you should also reject yourself or that you should think of yourself as a lesser person. It doesn't mean that nobody will ever love you anymore. Remember that only ONE person has rejected you at the moment, and it only hurt so much because to you, that person's opinion symbolized the opinion of the whole world, of God. **Joycelyn Soriano**

21. When we are in love, we are convinced nobody else will do. But as times goes, others do do, and often do do, much much better. **Coco J. Ginger**

22. Blessed are those with cracks in their broken heart because that is how the light gets in. **Shannon L. Alder**

23. Love can stretch you beyond what you feel you can endure. But you can, and you must get back to love and living! **Staci A. Welch-Bartley**

24. No matter how hard your heart is broken, the world doesn't stop for your grief. **FaraazKazi**

25. Sometimes, when one person is missing, the whole world seems depopulated. **Alphonse de Lamartine**

26. It's the love that goes through the hardest trials and survives that's worth having. **Katie Ashley**

27. Love can sometimes be magic. But magic can sometimes just be an illusion. **Javan**

28. When one door closes, another door opens; but we so often look so long and so regretfully upon the closed door, that we do not see the ones which open for us. **Alexander Graham Bell**

29. Never regret yesterday. Life is in you today, and you make your tomorrow. **L. Ron Hubbard**

30. I have lost and loved and won and cried myself to the person I am today. **Charlotte Eriksson**

CONCLUSION

"Getting over a painful experience is much like crossing monkey bars. You have to let go at some points in order to move forward," said C.S. Lewis.

Like I said at the beginning of this book, heartbreak in a love relationship is a very hurtful experience. It can be so devastating that it can tear the heart into pieces and makes the victim fall into the state of depression and stagnation in life.

However, this can only happen if you allow it.

Yes, show me someone who is enjoying a happy and meaningful relationship or marriage today and I will show you someone who had suffered the worst

119

form of disappointment or breakup in time past.

Dear reader, don't let an experience of heartbreak destroy you or place your life on hold. Although we don't pray for it, if it occurs, don't give room for self-pity, depression and regrets. Give God thanks in all circumstances as the Scripture says (See 1 Thess. 5:18).

I will conclude with this quote: **"When something bad happens, you have 3 choices. You can let it 1) define you, 2) destroy you and 3) strengthen you."** Now, I put it to you, which of these three choices will you make? I believe it is the third. You desire to be healed of your heart wounds and get strengthened up. Right? This is also my desire for you. I urge you therefore to follow these steps

120

and certainly, you will let me know that indeed, they work wonders.

God has helped me to share and also helped you to read. In your hand now lies 21-PLUS strategies to find strength to overcome and turn your pain of heartbreak into gain. Now, you have been empowered with the right knowledge to successfully pick up the broken pieces of your heart, put them together and make it whole again.

I therefore encourage you to take these 21 proven steps and everything you have learnt in this book so that you can enjoy the positive results they promise those who take them. I'm confident that if you do, your life will be more meaningful and fulfilled.

THE GOOD NEWS

The general aim of this book is to help you become a happy better version of yourself, achieve your highest potentials and live your best life. Beyond what you've just learnt in this book, here is something even more crucial to achieving your highest potentials and fulfilling the plan of God for your life.

Just before we part in our journey through the pages of this book, this is the ultimate good news for you. And the good news is, eternal life (true happiness and lasting success) has been restored to man through the death of His Son, Jesus Christ on the Cross.

What guarantees an enduring happiness and success in this world of great

122

corruption is, having a son or daughter/father relationship with God Almighty through His Son, Jesus Christ.

According to the Bible, (God's manual for our profitable living), we lost God's plan of total happiness and eternal life because of the sin of our first parents (Adam and Eve) in Eden. So, we were doomed – certain to suffer and die. But because of God's immeasurable love and grace for you and me, He sent His only Begotten Son, Jesus Christ to this sinful world to suffer and die in our place (See Isaiah 53:4). He did this so that those who believe and accept Jesus Christ will no more suffer or die, but enjoy a happy better life on earth here and then life eternal in Heaven (John 3:16).

Now the question is, "Have you accepted

Jesus Christ as your Lord and Personal Saviour?"

If 'Yes', then you have taken the best decision you can ever make in life. I encourage you to continue striving to maintain a close and holy relationship with God Almighty. No matter the painful experiences of life you face, refuse to lose trust in the Lord. Don't give up because in due season, you will reap the good fruits of your patience, obedience and trust in God, the faithful rewarder of those who diligently follow Him to the end (Gal. 6:9, Heb. 11:6).

But if your answer to the above question is 'No', then, no moment can be better than 'NOW' to do so. It's 'Now' because we humans don't have control over our time on this earth. In clearer words, this may be the only moment you have to make this most important decision you can ever make in your life. And, failure to make it NOW may cause you eternal regret and suffering in the lake where its fire never quenches and worms never die (Mark 9:48).

I encourage you to maximize this opportunity and never allow it to slip away as it may never come again.

If you are ready, then sincerely say this simple prayer below.

Lord Jesus, I come to you today. I open the door of my heart for you to come in. Forgive me my sins and save me from the curse of sin and death. From now on, I decide to follow you. In faith, I receive your gift of salvation to me. Lord, thank you for saving me, in Jesus' name. Amen!

125

Congratulations. I welcome you to the family of the Redeemed.

What is next?

Yes, to grow in your new way of life, you must identify yourself with other true believers by joining a Bible- believing church in your locality. And as instructed by Jesus Christ, the Author and Finisher of our faith, ensure you receive water baptism because without this, your salvation is not complete (John 3:1-7).

May the Grace of our Lord Jesus Christ, the Love of God and the Fellowship of the Holy Spirit remain with you, now and always in Jesus' name. Amen!

FINAL NOTE TO READER

Finally, Potential Carrier, my esteemed reader, thank you for buying this book and taking your time to read it to the end. I know that having read this book, you will become a happy better version of yourself, pursue your dreams and live your best life in the area of love relationship/marriage and generally in life.

Living your best life means the fulfilment of my God-given purpose on earth – helping people become the happy better version of themselves, unleash their fullest potentials and live their best life. And you know, nothing gives a man joy more than the fulfilment of his life purpose. Once more, thank you.

May God keep helping us daily grow into our happy better selves and fulfill His purposes for our lives in Jesus' name. Amen!

I want to hear from you; how this book has inspired you, helped you to recover from your heartbreak, and happily move on in life.

To connect with me, use any of the following channels:

Email: oghovemubooks@gmail.com

Facebook: www.facebook.com/oghovemuokpu

Instagram: @happybetteryou

Phone Number/WhatsApp: +237067441293

Also, to keep you going on the path of happiness and success in life, take time to visit my blogsite: www.HappyBetterYou.com or Facebook page: www.facebook.com/happybetteru and enjoy my life-transforming and inspirational articles, and other contents.

Disclaimer

This book and the content provided therein are simply for educational purposes and to serve as a guide to living the best of life, challenges notwithstanding.

The author does not bear responsibility for any result arising from the application of any information or idea contained in this book. You're taking full responsibility.

Thank you.

APPRECIATION

I register my profound gratitude: To the Almighty God, the source of my life; the one who gave me the knowledge, strength and inspiration to write this book. May His name be praise forever more. Amen!

To my beloved father in the Lord, Jesus' Holiness, Saint Dikeji Daniel MiyeriJesu, The Bishop of the Whole World. My happy and successful life today is the fruit of his consistent efforts through his teachings, prayers, hand of discipline, fatherly care and love. May God Almighty who called him continue to stand by him and cause him to finish successfully, the work He gave him to do on earth in Jesus' name. Amen!

To Ogheneochukome J. Eghaghara, Success Emonefe and Myra O. Oba for taking time to proofread this work. The corrections and

131

suggestions they made added more value to this work.

To my wonderful Facebook friend, Adeniyi Jamiu Bayonle for the big role he played in the publishing of this book, especially on Amazon.

To the members of the following Facebook groups or communities: Online Publishers and Entrepreneurs Network, Writers and Authors Promotions, Writers Helping Writers, and others whose suggestions and recommendations added colour to this book.

And once more, to you my esteemed reader for buying this book and taking your time to read it, a decision that means much to the fulfilment of our lives' purpose.

May God shower His blessings on you all in Jesus' name. Amen!

MEET THE AUTHOR

OGHOVEMU DANIEL OKPU is a life coach, public speaker, writer, publisher, an editor and expert in the field of human potential development.

His life purpose is to help individuals become the happy better version of themselves, unleash their fullest potentials and live their best life. He calls his readers potential carriers because he believes that they carry the inherent ability to improve their lives.

He is the Founder of Happy Better You www.happybetteryou.com, a personal development, educational and inspirational platform where he provides people with the information, resources and the inspiration they need to become happy and successful in life.

133

As a life coach, Daniel has helped many people throughtout the globe improve their lives through his coaching, speaking engagements, articles and books.

Daniel is passionate about encouraging the brokenhearted in every area of life and helping them to see challenges from a positive angle, a mindset which equip them with the strength to stay strong and finally overcome. It's this strong desire that moved him to write this book, "Healing Your Broken Heart."

He is a Christian and lover of God. He is single and currently lives in Warri, Nigeria.

OTHER BOOKS BY THE AUTHOR

 **IT'S FINISHED:** *How to Gain and Sustain Your Freedom in Christ and Use It to Fulfill God's Purpose for Your Life*

 **OVERCOMING YOUR HAPPINESS KILLERS:** *4 Common Habits that Steal Your Happiness, How to Crush them and Live Happy Everyday*

You can check them out on Amazon through this link: www.bit.ly/oghovemu

Now visit: www.happybetteryou.com